᷍ Mothers' Wit

Allison Vale & Alison Rattle

PRION

First published in Great Britain in 2008 by

Prion
an imprint of the
Carlton Publishing Group
20 Mortimer Street
London W1T 3JW

2 4 6 8 10 9 7 5 3 1

Some of the material in this book was
previously published in 2005 in *Mothers' Wit*

A catalogue record for this book is available from the British Library

ISBN 978-1-85375-650-4

Printed in Singapore

INTRODUCTION

If motherhood were easy it would not begin
with something called labour. Being a mum has
always been hard work: toddlers have always
been trouble, teenagers have always been foul,
and mothers-in-law have always been quick to
point out where you're going wrong. But from
the first sleepless days with a newborn to gawky,
malodorous and misunderstood adolescence, there
is one weapon a mother will rely on above all
others: her sense of humour.

In this collection of classic one-liners, a host of
celebrities extol the 'joys' of motherhood from
après-birth jelly-bellies and sick-covered nighties
to the hormonal teenager and the doting grandma.

'If you never want to see a man again, say, "I love you. I want to marry you. I want to have children" – they leave skid marks.'

Rita Rudner

'I want to have children and I know my time is running out. I want to have them while my parents are still young enough to take care of them.'

Rita Rudner

'My ultimate fantasy is to entice a man to my bedroom, put a gun to his head and say, "Make babies or die." '

Ruby Wax

'Advice to expectant mothers: you must remember that when you are pregnant you are eating for two. But you must also remember that the other one of you is about the size of a golf ball, so let's not go overboard with it. I mean a lot of pregnant women eat as though the other person they're eating for is Orson Welles.'

Dave Barry

'My obstetrician was so dumb that when I gave birth he forgot to cut the cord. For a year that kid followed me everywhere, it was like having a dog on a leash.'

Joan Rivers

'Don't tell your kids you had an easy birth or they won't respect you. For years I used to wake my daughter up and say, "Melissa, you ripped me to shreds. Now go back to sleep."'

Joan Rivers

'Watching a baby being born
is like watching a wet
St Bernard coming in through
the cat door.'

Jeff Foxworthy

'I haven't been thus shocked
since well I gave birth to you:
I thought you were wind,
I very nearly called you Fart.'

Linda, *Gimme, Gimme, Gimme*

'After you have a baby, in a few months you work your way up to getting dressed. Then, after a few more months, you can start doing your hair, maybe putting on makeup a few times. But you never, ever get back to accessorizing.'

Michelle Pfeiffer

'It's a huge change for your body. You don't even want to look in the mirror after you've had a baby, because you stomach is just hanging there like a Shar-Pei.'

Cindy Crawford

'You've been a fantastic mother. You've let them ruin your figure. Your stomach is stretched beyond recognition, you've got tits down to your knees and what for, for God's sake?'

Patsy to Edina, *Absolutely Fabulous*

'My kids always perceived the bathroom as a place where you wait it out until all the groceries are unloaded from the car.'

Erma Bombeck

'Children always understand.
They have open minds. They
have built-in shit detectors.'

Madonna

'Notoriously insensitive to subtle shifts in mood, children will persist in discussing the colour of a recently sighted cement mixer long after one's own interest in the topic has waned.'

Fran Lebowitz

'My mother's obsession with the good scissors always scared me a bit. It implied that somewhere in the house there lurked: the evil scissors.'

Tony Martin

'Spooky things happen in houses densely occupied by adolescent boys. When I checked out a four-inch dent in the living room ceiling one afternoon, even the kid still holding the baseball bat looked genuinely baffled about how he could possibly have done it.'

Mary Kay Blakely

'My teenage son is half-man, half-mattress.'

Val Valentine

'One thing they never tell you about childraising is that for the rest of your life, at the drop of a hat, you will be expected to know your child's name and how old he or she is.'

Erma Bombeck

'They're all mine…. Of course I'd trade any one of them for a dishwasher.'

Roseanne Barr

'Sometimes when I look at my children, I say to myself, "Lillian, you should have remained a virgin." '

Lillian Carter, mother of President
Jimmy Carter

'I used to be excellent. Since having a baby I couldn't tell you what day it is.'

Gwyneth Paltrow

'I'm eighteen years behind in my ironing. There's no use doing it now, it doesn't fit anybody I know.'

Phyllis Diller

'There will be other Mother's Days and a parade of gifts that will astound and amaze you, but not one of them will ever measure up to the sound of your children in the kitchen on Mother's Day whispering, "Don't you dare bleed on Mum's breakfast." '

Erma Bombeck

'Motherhood is having someone else to blame when there's a rude smell in the air.'

Jane Horrocks

'The first time you leave your child at school you're faced with a tough decision – down the pub or back to bed?'

Jo Brand

'Motherhood is perhaps the only unpaid position where failure to show up can result in arrest.'

Mary Kay Blakely

'Motherhood is not for the faint-hearted. Frogs, skinned knees and the insults of teenage girls are not for the wimpy.'

Danielle Steel

'Be nice to your children,
for they will choose your
rest home.'

Phyllis Diller

'I think motherhood makes you apathetic because you're always so tired. I don't know how anyone can march or be politically active when they've only had three hours' sleep.'

Jo Brand

'I like trying to get pregnant. I'm not so sure about childbirth.'

George Eliot

'Life is tough enough without having someone kick you from the inside.'

Rita Rudner

'Giving birth is like taking you lower lip and forcing it over your head.'

Carole Burnett

'If men had to have babies
they would only ever have
one each.'

Princess Diana

'Our planning may leave something to be desired, but our designs, thanks God, have been flawless.'

Noor, Queen of Jordan, having given birth to her fourth child in six years

'The breasts go first,
and then the waist and then
the butt. Nobody ever tells
you that you get a butt when
you get pregnant.'

Elle Macpherson

'Do not, on a rainy day, ask your child what he feels like doing, because I assure you that what he feels like doing, you won't feel like watching.'

Fran Lebowitz

'Children ask better questions than adults. "May I have a cookie?" "Why is the sky blue?" and "What does a cow say?" are far more likely to elicit a cheerful response than "Where is your manuscript?" "Why haven't you called?" and "Who's your lawyer?" '

Fran Lebowitz

'I've seen kids ride bicycles, run, play ball, set up a camp, swing, fight a war, swim and race for eight hours... yet have to be driven to the garbage can.'

Erma Bombeck

'It's always been my feeling that God lends you your children until they are about 18 years old. If you haven't made your point with them by then, it's too late.'

Betty Ford

'The best way to keep children at home is to make the atmosphere pleasant, and let the air out of the tyres.'

Dorothy Parker

'Mothers are inclined to feel limp at 50. This is because the children have taken most of her stuffing to build their nests.'

Samantha Armstrong

'Wrinkles are hereditary.
Parents get them from
their children.'

Mae West

' If your baby is beautiful and perfect, never cries or fusses, sleeps on schedule and burps on demand, an angel all the time, you're the grandma.'

Theresa Bloomingdale

'My grandmother was a very tough woman. She buried three husbands and two of them were just napping.'

Rita Rudner

'I hope you all saved room, because I made your favourite dessert. Store-bought snack cakes – both kinds.'

Marge, *The Simpsons*

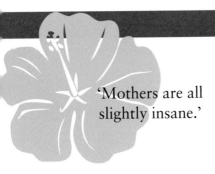

'Mothers are all
slightly insane.'

J. D. Salinger

'How do you know if it's time to wash the dishes and clean your house? Look inside your pants. If you find a penis in there, it's not time.'

Jo Brand

'My second-favourite household chore is ironing. My first being hitting my head on the top bunk until I faint.'

Erma Bombeck

'Neurotics build castles in the air, psychotics live in them. My mother cleans them.'

Rita Rudner

'I'm sitting on the toilet and I'm looking at the grouting on the tiles, that grouting really gets me. Mothers have a thing about grouting.'

Sharon Osbourne

'There's something wrong with a mother who washes out a measuring cup with soap and water after she's only measured water in it.'

Erma Bombeck

'I will clean the house when Sears come out with a riding vacuum cleaner.'

Roseanne Barr

'No one knows what her life expectancy is, but I have a horror of leaving this world and not having anyone in the entire family know how to replace a toilet tissue spindle.'

Erma Bombeck

'I may be the only mother in America who knows exactly what their child is up to all the time.'

Barbara Bush

'I'm a mother with two small children, so I don't take as much crap as I used to.'

Pamela Anderson

'Children reinvent your world
for you.'

Susan Sarandon

'Be a first-rate version of yourself, not a second-rate version of someone else.'

Judy Garland
to her daughter, Liza Minelli

'There is nothing more thrilling in this world, I think, than having a child that is yours, and yet is mysteriously a stranger.'

Agatha Christie

'I love all my children, but some of them I don't like.'

Lillian Carter, mother of President Jimmy Carter

'Don't call me an icon. I'm just a mother trying to help.'

Princess Diana

'I was not a classic mother. But my kids were never palmed off to boarding school. So I didn't bake cookies. You can buy cookies but you can't buy love.'

Raquel Welch

'The easiest way to convince my kids that they don't really want something is to get it for them.'

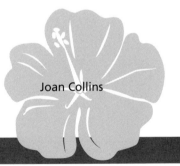

Joan Collins

'I want to spend more time with my family but I'm not sure they want to spend time with me.'

Esther Rantzen

'I am not Superwoman. The reality of my daily life is that I'm juggling a lot of balls in the air… and sometimes some of the balls get dropped.'

Cherie Blair

'The great high of winning Wimbledon lasts for about a week. You go down in the record book, but you don't have anything tangible to hold on to. But having a baby – there isn't any comparison.'

Chris Evert Lloyd

'I don't like waving my children like a celebrity trophy. I know everyone wants to see if they're fat and look like me.'

Jo Brand

'I have come, Sire, to complain of one of your subjects who has been so audacious as to kick me in the belly.'

Marie Antoinette, telling Louis XVI of France that she was pregnant with their first child

'My mother's great. She has all the major looks. She could stop you from doing anything, through a closed door even, with a single look. Without saying a word, she has that power to rip out your tonsils.'

Whoopi Goldberg

'My mother used to say there
are no strangers, only friends
you haven't met yet. She's
now in a maximum security
twilight home in Australia.'

Dame Edna Everage

'After my mother I never needed anyone else.'

Mae West

'An ugly baby is a very nasty object – and the prettiest is frightful.'

Queen Victoria

'Children should be like
waffles... you should be able
to throw the first one away.'

Nancy Mitford

'I don't know how to do anything – I'm a mom.'

Roseanne Barr

'Level with your child by being honest. Nobody spots a phony quicker than a child.'

Mary MacCracken

'Experts say you should never hit your children in anger. When is a good time? When you're feeling festive?'

Roseanne Barr

'If you raise three children who can knock out and hog tie a perfect stranger, you must be doing something right.'

Marge, *The Simpsons*

'When my kids become unruly, I use a nice, safe playpen. When they're finished I climb out.'

Erma Bombeck

'I don't believe in smacking
– I use a cattle prod.'

Jenny Éclair

'You couldn't fool your mother in the foolingest day of your life if you had an electrified fooling machine.'

Homer, *The Simpsons*

'My mom said the only
reason men are alive
is for lawn care and
vehicle maintenance.'

Tim Allen

'Don't forget Mother's Day.
Or as they call it in Beverly
Hills, Dad's Third Wife Day.'

Jay Leno

'There is nothing a mother likes better than breakfast in bed – cold toast, burned scrambled eggs and a newly picked rose dripping dew and greenfly into the cornflakes.'

Peter Gray

'Whenever I'm with my mother, I feel as though I have to spend the whole time avoiding land mines.'

Amy Tan

'Life began with waking up
and loving my mother's face.'

George Eliot

'A sweater is a garment worn by the child when the mother feels chilly.'

Barbara Johnson

'Even when freshly washed and relieved of all obvious confections, children tend to be sticky.'

Fran Lebowitz

'Being a child is horrible.
It is slightly better than being
a tree or a piece of heavy
machinery but not half as
good as being a domestic cat.'

Julie Burchill

'Toddlers are more likely
to eat healthy food if they
find it on the floor.'

Jan Blaustone

'There never was a child so lovely, but his mother was glad to get him asleep.'

Ralph Waldo Emerson

'Over the years I have learned that motherhood is much like an austere religious order, the joining of which obligates one to relinquish all claims to personal possessions.'

Nancy Stahl

'I remember opening the refrigerator late one night and finding [I had chilled] a roll of aluminium foil next to a pair of small red tennis shoes.... I quickly closed the door and ran upstairs to make sure I had put the babies in their cribs instead of the linen closet.'

Mary Kay Blakely

'You never realize how much your mother loves you till you explore the attic – and find every letter you ever sent her, every finger painting, clay pot, bead necklace, Easter chicken, cardboard Santa Claus, paperlace Mother's Day card and school report since day one.'

Pam Brown

'Now the thing about having a baby – and I can't be the first person to have noticed this – is that thereafter you have it.'

Jean Kerr

'Being a housewife and mother is the biggest job in the world, but if it doesn't interest you don't do it – I would have made a terrible mother.'

Katharine Hepburn

'I never used to like babies. I mean, I'd always think, "Well if a baby were more like a chimpanzee, I'd have one." '

Candice Bergen

'Think of stretch marks as pregnancy service stripes.'

Joyce Armor

'I was horrified to find myself being described as a geriatric mother who, by the time my child had reached school age, would have a brain like a soggy rusk and would have the personality and mobility of a stuffed parrot.'

Jan Anderson, on pregnancy in her forties

'I realize why women die in childbirth – it's preferable.'

Sherry Glaser

'A suburban mother's role is to deliver children obstetrically once, and by car for ever after.'

Peter DeVries

'Poverty is a lot like childbirth – you know it is going to hurt before it happens, but you'll never know how much until you experience it.'

Joanne Kathleen Rowling

'Giving birth was easier than having a tattoo.'

Nicole Appleton

'When I was giving birth the nurse asked, "Still think blondes have more fun?" '

Joan Rivers

'Childbirth classes neglect to teach one critical skill: how to breathe, count and swear all at the same time.'

Linda Fiterman

'I'd be happy to stand next to any man I know in one of those labour rooms the size of a Volkswagen and whisper, "No dear, you don't really need the Demerol; just relax and do your second-stage breathing." '

Anna Quindlen

'Birth control that really works:
every night before we go to bed
we spend an hour with our kids.'

Roseanne Barr

'Most men cannot change a
diaper without subsequently
renting an aeroplane that
trails a banner which says,
"I CHANGED A DIAPER".'

Anna Quindlen

'Children see everything
according to how it impinges
on them.'

Nigella Lawson

'A child develops individuality long before he develops taste. I have seen my kid straggle into the kitchen in the morning with outfits that need only one accessory: an empty gin bottle.'

Erma Bombeck

'If you have never been hated
by your child you have never
been a parent.'

Bette Davis

'If your mother tells you to do a thing, it is wrong to reply that you won't. It is better and more becoming to intimate that you will do as she bids you, and then afterwards act quietly in the matter according to the dictates of your better judgement.'

Mark Twain

'When you're sitting at home with sick all over your nightie, it's great to be able to do something which means you don't have to go out.'

Jo Brand, on writing her first book

'All mothers think their children are oaks, but the world never lacks for cabbages.'

Robertson Davies

'I would be most content
if my children grew up
to be the kind of people
who think decorating
consists mostly of building
enough bookshelves.'

Anna Quindlen

'One day my mother called me… and she said, "Forty-nine million Americans saw you on television tonight. One of them is the father of my future grandchild, but he's never going to call you because you wore your glasses." '

Lesley Stahl, newsreader

'Until I got married, when
I used to go out, my mother
used to say goodbye to me as
though I was emigrating.'

Thora Hird

'Nothing looks as lonely as your mom before she sees you coming up the platform.'

Pam Brown

'Kids are cute, babies are cute, puppies are cute. The little things are cute. See, nature did this on purpose so that we would want to take care of our young. Made them cute, tricked us. Then gradually they get older and older, until one day your mother sits you down and says, "You know, I think you're ugly enough to get your own apartment." '

Cathy Ladman

'I refuse to admit that
I am more than 52,
even if that does make my
sons illegitimate.'

Nancy Astor

'My theory on housework is, if the item doesn't multiply, smell, catch fire, or block the refrigerator door, let it be. No one else cares. Why should you?'

Erma Bombeck

'I hate housework! You make the beds, you do the dishes – and six months later you have to start all over again.'

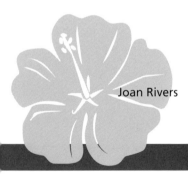

Joan Rivers

'I love acting but it's much
more fun taking the kids
to the zoo.'

Nicole Kidman

'I don't have a nanny or a housekeeper, and only have a cleaner for one hour each week. I finish work and go home, I cook the dinner. I run into Tesco and do the housework in the evening.'

Victoria Beckham

'Never have more children
than you have car windows.'

Erma Bombeck

'The story of a mother's life:
Trapped between a scream
and a hug.'

Cathy Guisewite

'Motherhood is like Albania –
you can't trust the brochures,
you have to go there.'

Marni Jackson

'There's a lot more to being a woman than being a mother, but there's a lot more to being a mother than most people suspect.'

Roseanne Barr

'The trouble with mothers is that however well groomed and sophisticated you appear to strangers, they know your knickers are probably held up with a safety pin.'

Samantha Armstrong

'My husband and I are either going to buy a dog or have a child. We can't decide whether to ruin our carpet or ruin our lives.'

Rita Rudner

'It would seem that something which means poverty, disorder and violence every single day should be avoided entirely, but the desire to beget children is a natural urge.'

Phyllis Diller

'Having children is what
a woman is born for really.'

Nastassja Kinski

'I get those maternal feelings. Like when I'm lying on the couch and can't reach the remote. "Boy, a kid would be nice, right now." '

Kathleen Madigan

'Women who miscalculate are called mothers.'

Abigail Van Buren

'By far the most common
craving of pregnant women
is not to be pregnant.'

Phyllis Diller

'My sister was in labour for thirty-six hours. Ow! She got wheeled out of the delivery, looked at me and said, "Adopt." '

Caroline Rhea

'Birthday parties are a lot like childbirth. After both events you swear you'll never make that mistake again.'

Linda Fiterman

'A baby's a full-time job for three adults. Nobody tells you that when you're pregnant, or you'd probably jump off a bridge.'

Erica Jong

'Children seldom misquote you. They more often repeat word for word what you shouldn't have said.'

Mae Maloo

'There is no reciprocity.
Men love women, women
love children. Children
love hamsters.'

Alice Thomas Ellis

'Youngsters of the age of two
or three are endowed with
extraordinary strength.
They can lift a dog twice their
own weight and dump him
in the bathtub.'

Erma Bombeck

'Kids can be a pain in the neck when they're not a lump in your throat.'

Barbara Johnson

'There is only one pretty child in the world, and every mother has it.'

Chinese proverb

'Before I became a mother I was such a free spirit. I used to say, "No man will ever dominate me." Now I have a six-year-old master.'

Sally Diaz

'Parents of young children should realize that few people, and maybe no one, will find their children as enchanting as they do.'

Barbara Walters

'The easiest way for your children to learn about money is for you not to have any.'

Katharine Whitehorn

'The reason you want your children to pay attention in school is you haven't the faintest idea how to do their homework.'

Hazel Scott

'A mother is neither cocky, nor proud, because she knows the school principal may call at any minute to report that her child has just driven a motorcycle through the gymnasium.'

Mary Kay Blakely

'Never lend your car
to anyone to whom you have
given birth.'

Erma Bombeck

'Oh, to be only half
as wonderful as my child
thought I was when he was
small, and only half as stupid
as my teenager now thinks
I am.'

Rebecca Richards

'Well it is every mother's dream to get a good look at her daughter's boyfriend's package.'

Roseanne, *Roseanne*

'Alligators have the right idea.
They eat their young.'

Eve Arden

'My daughter thinks I'm nosy. At least that's what she says in her diary.'

Sally Poplin

' "Working mother" is a misnomer…. It implies that any mother without a definite career is lolling around eating bon-bons, reading novels, and watching soap opera.'

Liz Smith

'I want my children to have all the things I couldn't afford. Then I want to move in with them.'

Phyllis Diller

'It kills you to see them grow up. But I guess it would kill you quicker if they didn't.'

Barbara Kingsolver

'I take a very practical view
of raising children;
I put a sign in each of their
rooms: checkout time
is eighteen years.'

Erma Bombeck

'Most children threaten to run away from home. This is the only thing that keeps some parents going.'

Phyllis Diller

'Ask your child what he wants for dinner only if he is buying.'

Fran Lebowitz

'My kids keep trying to convince me that there are two separate parts of their stomachs, one dedicated to dinner and the other to dessert.'

Anna Quindlen

'How to eat like a child: divide spinach into little piles. Rearrange again into new piles. After five or six manoeuvres, sit back and say you're full.'

Delia Ephron

'All of us have moments in our lives that test our courage. Taking children into a house with a white carpet is one of them.'

Erma Bombeck

'Cleaning the house while the kids are still growing is like shovelling the walk before it stops snowing.'

Phyllis Diller

'A sparkling house is a fine thing if the children aren't robbed of their lustre in keeping it that way.'

Marcelene Cox

'Now as always, the most automated appliance in a household is the mother.'

Beverly Jones

'Children are the most desirable opponents at Scrabble as they are both easy to beat and fun to cheat.'

Fran Lebowitz

'Sing out loud in the car even,
or especially, if it embarrasses
the children.'

Marilyn Penland

'I was doing the family grocery shopping accompanied by two children, an event I hope to see included in the Olympics in the near future.'

Anna Quindlen

'I'm a godmother,
that's a great thing to be
a godmother. She calls me
God for short, that's cute,
I taught her that.'

Ellen DeGeneres

'An advantage to having one
child is you always know
who did it.'

Baba Bell Hajdusiewicz

'Children and zip fasteners
do not respond to force…
except occasionally.'

Katharine Whitehorn

'The hardest people to convince they are at retirement age are children at bedtime.'

Shannon Fife

'Hotdogs always seem better
out than at home, so do
French fried potatoes;
so do your children.'

Mignon McLaughlin

'The best time to start giving
your children money is when
they will no longer eat it.'

Barbara Coloroso